RUSH OF WINGSPAN

THE HUGH MacLENNAN POETRY SERIES
Editors: Allan Hepburn and Carolyn Smart

Rush of Wingspan

ELEONORE SCHÖNMAIER

McGill-Queen's University Press
Montreal & Kingston • London • Chicago

© Eleonore Schönmaier 2026

ISBN 978-0-2280-2716-4 (paper)
ISBN 978-0-2280-2717-1 (ePDF)
ISBN 978-0-2280-2718-8 (ePUB)

Legal deposit first quarter 2026
Bibliothèque et Archives nationales du Québec

Printed in Canada on acid-free paper that is 100% ancient-forest-free, containing 100% sustainable, recycled fibre, and processed chlorine-free.

We acknowledge the support of the Canada Council for the Arts.
Nous remercions le Conseil des arts du Canada de son soutien.

McGill-Queen's University Press in Montreal is on land which long served as a site of meeting and exchange amongst Indigenous Peoples, including the Haudenosaunee and Anishinabeg nations. In Kingston it is situated on the territory of the Haudenosaunee and Anishinaabek. We acknowledge and thank the diverse Indigenous Peoples whose footsteps have marked these territories on which peoples of the world now gather.

Library and Archives Canada Cataloguing in Publication

Title: Rush of wingspan / Eleonore Schönmaier.

Names: Schönmaier, Eleonore, author

Series: Hugh MacLennan poetry series.

Description: Series statement: The Hugh MacLennan poetry series

Identifiers: Canadiana (print) 20250255510 | Canadiana (ebook) 20250255510 | ISBN 9780228027164 (softcover) | ISBN 9780228027171 (PDF) | ISBN 9780228027188 (ePUB)

Subjects: LCGFT: Poetry.

Classification: LCC PS8587.C4585 R87 2026 | DDC C811/.54—dc23

This book was designed and typeset by Marquis Interscript in 9.5/13 Sabon.
Copyediting by Nina Ballerstedt.

McGill-Queen's University Press
Suite 1720, 1010 Sherbrooke St West, Montreal, QC, H3A 2R7

Authorized safety representative in the EU: Mare Nostrum Group BV, Mauritskade 21D, 1091 GC Amsterdam, the Netherlands, gpsr@mare-nostrum.co.uk

For Bruce, always

and

in memory of
Hannah Wertheim

CONTENTS

NORTHERN BUSH

Understatements 3
Counting 4
Visible 5
Pretending 6
Overburden 7
Fields 8
Thawing 9
When Southerners Ask About the Animals 10
Lamplight 11
Surfaces 12
Weasels 13
Newspaper Girl 14
Wallet 15
Babysitter 16
Party 17
Into the Garden 18
Traces 19
Reaches 20
Swimming 21
Untouched 22
Candy Striper 24
Rumours 25
Security 27
The Library in the Winter 28
Flight into Puppetry 30
Census Taker 32
Ashes 34
Taiga 36

On the Line   37
Tools   38
Penelope   39

ATLANTIC COASTAL FOREST

Ancestors   43
Keening   44
Straying   45
Sun-Warmed   47
This Painting Not Yet Hung on the Wall   48
Lullaby   49
Naturally   50
Kindness   51
Riverbeds   52
Joining Us in the Water   54
La Main   55
Burning   56
Floats   58

NORTH SEA CITY FOREST

Barn Owls   61
Black Earth   63
Midnight   65
Rhododendron Bush   67
Sunlight   68
The Long Marriage   69
Trains Still Arrive   70
Reunion of Two Lovers   71
Lanterns   72
Much Depends Upon   73
Late   74

WINGS

When Wings Open Doors   77
Windows   79
Chance   80
Wings of Voorlinden   82
When the Salons Are Shuttered   84
Over the Edge   85
The Starving   86
Dawning of Dusk
  Morning   87
  Afternoon   88
  Night   89

GEOMETRIES OF LIGHT

Zoo   93
Star Silt   95
Leiden   97
Blue Light   99
Windowpanes   101
Glint   103
Geometries of Light   104
The Lining   106
Yield   108
Grieving   109
Bowl   110
Clarity   111

NIGHT ALIGNMENTS

Tending   115
Night Alignments   116
Bloom   117
These Are the Objects   118

Secret Code 119
Blackbirds and Greenfinches 121
Inventory 123
History 124
Enter 125
Hesitations 126
Blur 128
At Play 129
Model Collapse 130
What Is Left Is 131
Shape 132
Sculpture 133

ENTANGLEMENTS

Bodies of Work 137
Art Options 139
The Unwritten Book 140
Starstruck 141
Animals 144
Sailor
  When a Friend Lends a Poet Movies 146
  When Love Is an Incinerator 147
  Great Circle Route 149
  All Lit Up 151
  While Kissing Onboard 152
Shore Leave
  Rain 153
  The Bliss of Storm Eccentricities 154
  Fleeting 155
Open Gates 156

Acknowledgments 159
Notes 163

NORTHERN BUSH

UNDERSTATEMENTS

My father's oldest
sister is about
to visit. He writes

*We're not poor
but we're living
in poverty.*

When she arrives
ants rain down from
the bedroom ceiling

into her curly hair.
She never returns
and writes, *How*

can you live like this?

COUNTING

With no English
I start school
and when I fail

to count to five
I'm forced
to spend time

in the cloak room
where I feel
a fur collar

brush against
my face
in the darkness.

VISIBLE

My father buys
my first and only
bike, an adult

model
for my sixth
birthday.

I race
to school
on the gravel road

and the scars
on my knees
are visible

decades later
under the hem
of my skirt.

PRETENDING

I walk through the dense
bush to an overhang
of rock

on the pond's edge
where I wait
for my friends. We pole

our raft out into the deep
of the water
and we pretend

if one of us falls off
into the mine tailings
murk, we'll be dead.

OVERBURDEN

For thousands of years
Tom's family
have lived in the boreal forest

and today in school
he tells me how the mine
dumped toxic tailings

that flooded right up
to the doorstep of
his grandmother's house.

FIELDS

On the cyanide field
I'm part of the boys' soccer team
cause I can run

fast, faster, fastest
but I can't outrun
bruised shins

when the boys
miss the ball
and after practice

my face is adorned
with purple
when I'm pushed

into the pink
stucco
school wall.

THAWING

My father prepares
for spring, and wants
to transport the canoe

down to the lake.
Instead of portaging
the heavy weight

on his shoulders
he turns the canoe
into a sled.

He pulls from the bow
and I ride in the stern
coasting downhill

over the ice-coated
snow
through the forest.

We reach the frozen
water, and we're ready
for spring.

WHEN SOUTHERNERS ASK ABOUT THE ANIMALS

When a black
bear crosses
my path

I stand still
and wait.
He sways

his furry butt
and lumbers past.
We share

the blueberries
but I know
he's the boss.

LAMPLIGHT

At dusk the moose
is at the side of
the road, high

as a wall.
Her eyes glint
in my bike's lamplight

but she stays
still while I race
past at top speed.

SURFACES

At Halfway Creek
I see the V-shaped wake
as the beaver

swims towards his twig-mud
house. He'll only slap
his tail

against the surface
of the water
if I'm a threat

but I'm quieter
than the poplar tree
bending in the breeze.

WEASELS

I'm ten and my father
takes me into the bush
and will write his sister

that we travelled
for twenty-five kilometres
on foot

moving like weasels.
Do weasels walk that far?
I believe in angels

and visualize
them lifting up
the trail

like a piece of string.
They snip out a large section,
mend the remnants

seamlessly together,
and lay the shortened trail
back down on the earth

so I don't have to walk
as far, but can still travel
all the way.

NEWSPAPER GIRL

I'm eleven when
I paint my sled
white and call her

Suzy Snowflake.
I haul her up and down
the frozen streets.

She carries the newspapers
on her back
and she never

complains. When
I have time she also
lets me ride her down

the long hill
all the way
to the lake.

WALLET

As a preteen on a trip
into town
Christmas shopping

I have only a ten
dollar bill
from my paper route

plus my library card.
Placing my hand into
my pocket

I find the wallet
gone. But my mother
working

in the grocery store
gets a call from the Snake Pit.
I found your kid's wallet.

*Come get it
before I drink
it away.*

BABYSITTER

The child and I sit on the sofa
staring at the broken wooden box
with its glass face. We don't have other
people's stories to distract us in flashing
black and white images. Nor are there
toys. In the side room is a single bed
where the child and her absent
mother sleep. In the kitchen
I search the cupboards for
food, but even when I look
twice I find not a single
crumb. With imagination
and laughter we run
between the two
rooms.

PARTY

A boy starts
talking about
Moped Fred

who rides each day
to the mine
on two wheels

while all the macho
men whizz by
in pickup trucks.

There's a lot
of laughter
and I whisper

*His name is not
Fred and he's
my father.*

INTO THE GARDEN

My mother wakes
in the middle
of the night

to hear rain
hitting the bottom
of a tin bucket

but it only takes
her seconds
to realize

the sound
is peapods falling
into a pail.

She races out
into the garden while
the adept thief

leaps over the fence
vanishing into the bush
bucket and all.

TRACES

Our teacher wears
miniskirts
and tells us to lie down

on rolled out
butcher paper
so we can trace

ourselves and turn
our bodies
into art.

REACHES

I cycle the ten
bush-road clicks into town
and on the main street

a car coasts
right up next to me.
I focus

on my balance
and stay upright
as his arm reaches out

and circles my waist.
I don't look at him
as he pushes me ever so

slightly, ever so gently
just to make his point:
I could if I wanted to—

SWIMMING

I'm out there again
in the lake's middle when
the helicopter shows up

and hovers above my head.
Ok, so I'm wearing a hat,
glasses and am swimming

an awkward breaststroke as if
I just fell out of a boat,
as if I'm trying to reach

the shore. The hatch is open
and I can see the men up
there, kneeling, watching me.

Are they intent on kidnap or
rescue? I want to give them
the finger but focus straight

ahead to where the granite
glistens in the morning
light, the green fleck of

my summer dress
and my white
sneakers.

UNTOUCHED

Our school bus driver
says her friend needs
a weekend cleaner

for his tourist camp.
                    I scrub
the meat-blood stains

from the bottom of the fridge
while the owner's son cleans
the fish

and neatly slices
open
his right palm.

On a rare Sunday
the son flies me home
in his two-seater Cessna.

I look down at the field
of fireweed
the charcoaled trees

the clear-cuts
and the fresh-green
where the bush remains

untouched.
We circle the lake
scanning for boulders

and land smooth
as a bird. I walk through
the bush toward home.

CANDY STRIPER

I run as I cross over
the road between
my high school

and the hospital. I must feed
a toddler and watch over
a stroke patient. After I clean

the child's face I hold
her hand as we enter
the elderly man's room.

He drops a pillow
and as I bend over
the toddler grabs

a cabinet by the handle
and it crashes onto
the floor

missing the child
by a fraction. As I hold
her in my arms she calms

and we stare out
at the bush that stretches
beyond our reach.

RUMOURS

I'm on the tree planting
crew with the bible
thumpers. In the van

on the way to the clear-cut
I'm asked, *Have you found
Jesus?* During the long

day, what we haven't found
is a safe and discreet way
to empty our bladders.

The edge of the clear-cut
is too far away
and we're not to reveal

any bare skin. Dehydration
is the only
option. With my spade

I cut an "L"
into the ground
and gently set

a spruce seedling
into the corner
over and over over—

There are rumours
about another crew
the boozers

who work shirt-less
and are fully tanned
breasts and all.

SECURITY

In a photo taken by
the security guard
I'm sixteen and wearing

a green hard hat, filthy T-shirt
jeans and steel-toed boots.
Behind me is a flaking

concrete wall. In my hands
I hold a gold brick.
Later I'll frame

the image and place
it on the bookshelf.
When visitors come

my roommate turns
the picture face down.
Her studio

portrait captured
her in a party
dress. I say my photo

shows the only time
in my life when
I'll ever hold

a million dollars
in my bare
hands.

THE LIBRARY IN THE WINTER

Evenings and Saturdays
I'm there alone
as the assistant though

there's not much to assist.
The library is two rooms
above the bus station

and the bus station is one room
on the ground floor
with no buses. There are

a few vans and cars.
There are a few regular
routes where people

jam into the vans and
cars, and if you have money
(which most people don't)

you can get a car to be
your cab. Generally
the bus stop is a hangout

for drunks who get lost
and find their way
up to the library where

they may or may not read
the magazines. Occasionally
friends drop by: two boys

who want me to go
to the school
dance when I'm finished

working. One is drunk
and the other stoned. If
we show up at school

they'll be expelled
and school will be
even lonelier.

FLIGHT INTO PUPPETRY

I make a pilot and a plane
out of felt and hang
this in the library window

hoping to attract
children, but
each summer afternoon

when I teach
the program
an old bush pilot

comes in to read
the flight mags. Today's
lesson is finger puppets

and I deliberately make
the tiny toys into
sailors. Perhaps

I should have named
the program
Sailing into Puppetry.

I dream of the ocean
as I sit in the hot library
minus air conditioning

my cotton skirt
sticking to my bare
legs. The only ocean

visible is the inflatable
child's pool
on a storybook cover.

CENSUS TAKER

At eighteen I'm allocated
the edge of town and walk
on cliff tops where

it's hard to build. I face
a row of houses:
asphalt-shingled walls.

A man waves
his shotgun, *I'm drunk. Come
back tomorrow*—At the last

house I ask, *Are there any
more homes?*
The woman says, *No.*

I follow
the footpath
into the bush and find

a shelter of rough-hewn boards.
Twelve people. Wood nailed together
for two beds.

No chairs. An empty tin
of baked beans on the floor.
No bathroom. No income. No

birth dates.
        One more home.
A topple of boards touch

to form walls. A red
paper nailed to the door:
Condemned Unfit for Human

Habitation. I knock
and enter. No windows
only chinks in the walls.

My eyes slowly
adjust. A massive old
woman on the bed.

She gestures
for me to leave
the form. Outside

I look over
the cliff edge
down upon

the shore bungalows.
There the people
will yell

at me. They have numbers
they don't want
to share.

ASHES

Cooling water
hangs as virga: gauzy
streamers vanishing mid-air
        as the rain
fails to find
the earth during
my eighteenth year.
        Again and again
lightning
skewers the treetops.
        Flames.
Ashes as confetti
as flakes
of old newsprint.

Flown south
in a windowless
military jet, I'm unable
to see what's happening
to the forest.

In the city I stroll
among tombstones
to the famous

read plaques
for torn-down houses
but in the enormous

parking lots
the builders forgot
to imprint the names:

                         hemlock
chanterelle
          wolf lichen
                         quillwort
trout lily—

TAIGA

After the evacuation
order ended, we returned
home to discover
the forest reduced to black

ash. This wasn't surprising:
insurmountable flames
had reached hot and high.
The fire crept to the very edge of

all our memories. Unexpected
were the green-gentle shoots
that grew so soon after:

the forest already, slowly
starting to rise up, feeding
from the ash.

ON THE LINE

In the bush I'm alone
on my cross-country skis
and I know if I break

my leg it will be the guys
on their Ski-doos
with guns slung over

their shoulders who will stop
and rescue me. Back home
my neighbour's up his ladder

when I ask him if he'll sign
my petition to save the land.
He looks down at me and says

They'll burn your house down
but in his clear script he signs
his name on the line.

TOOLS

A boy falls off his bike. His brain
bleeds, and the doctor only has moments
to save him, but in the bush

there's no neurological
drill. From the maintenance
room he grabs a household

drill and he aims correctly
at the skull, and guesses how deep
to go. When the impossible

is necessary we can try
to attain it: there in front of us
is our room of tools: they're never the right

size or form, only mere approximations
but placed in our hands in the time
of greatest need if we drill not too deeply

we too (once or twice in our lives) may save
all that we wish to save, reach what we need to reach
so that the blood clot comes loose

and the brainwaves of strangers or
our own mind brimming can continue
in ways we had never imagined.

PENELOPE

As I'm pulling on my high
boots, my lover corrects
my pronunciation

when I tell him the author
I'll study today
is Penelope Fitzgerald.

Oh, I say. *I visualized
it differently.*
I'm skilled

in mispronouncing words
and names
in all my three

major languages (more if
you count the ones
I'm still learning).

I don't dare ask, *Is music
a language?* Words
on the page are silent.

They don't teach me
how to speak, they teach me how
to listen, how to think. On many

days I study on the shore
and wait for all the words
in all their sounds and songs

to sail home to me. This
takes years and some
bright sails as they billow

in the wind
I only ever hear
from a great distance.

ATLANTIC COASTAL FOREST

ANCESTORS

A day after heavy rain
I stand at just the right
angle and find a forest

mirror—this physics of light
where the sky-blue, leaf
green, and limbs of the trees

reflect from the pool
of water in the hollow
stump of an ancestor.

KEENING

The coastal road unspools
past goldfinches
flitting in and out

of the brush. I'm cycling
and suddenly
feel the pavement move

up through my bones
when trucks loaded
with lumber rattle by.

Slowly I regain
my balance and race
downhill. Arriving

in my forest home, I find
my neighbour's cottage
dangling in the air

shifted like a toy
to a different site.
Three new rooflines

rise across the harbour
where the fallen trees
will keen in the walls

of fresh wood
during bitter
winter nights.

STRAYING

From my back door
we enter the forest
along invisible pathways

that I sense with my feet
as we head
towards the sea.

We bend under boughs
and step out
onto the granite

of the shore.
The Atlantic Ocean
is wave-wild

in our ears.
We struggle over
boulders

and rest
on water-polished stone. Heading
back we slip

into the forest
and my lover
finally says, *How did you know*

to turn precisely there? I search
for this map so deeply
engraved in my thoughts

it's as if he'd asked me how
I breathe:
the curve of

landscape, the way
the light is falling
at this time of day.

SUN-WARMED

Wave-clinked together
as ocean pebbles

we're no longer solitary
in our pursuits:

this curved
sun-warmed

afternoon of conversing
as life channels

through us
on its way—

THIS PAINTING NOT YET HUNG
ON THE WALL

The rains with their heels knock
hard against the windowpanes.
The room with its low, sloped ceiling

is a tent tied fast. Yesterday
we tugged the sheets
from the summer line

and made up the bed:
a futon on a pine frame.
In the room's southwest corner

rest a beeswax candle
and a seashell from Portugal.
Abandoned

on the floor:
one pillow and
three matching socks.

LULLABY

What are the trees
with their skyline of branches
but roots that hold

us close to the earth? Yet every
night you wrench
me loose, or is it I who ride

your human limbs
so hard that by early
morning I need to rush

to the window to catch
the first light
as it reaches

into the forest.

NATURALLY

You pluck a small
spruce twig
covered in old

man's beard
from my
nightgown

and say, *Where
have you been
sleepwalking?*

KINDNESS

Our few possessions
in this home

that has no closets.
Crockery

and clothes
all on display.

The trees knock
against the north side

and a flicker
knocks from

inside the woodstove.
And it's true:

the door opens
daily.

RIVERBEDS

Both thought and wildlife
are parched. It hasn't rained
in four weeks. A squirrel

scampers its way
into the bedroom
both of us equally startled.

Deer crash through the brush
near the old dug well. And who
would have guessed in spring

that by July we would dance
for no other pleasure
but rain? The cloudless sky

is a glass ceiling trapping
us too close to ourselves.
In the lake our bodies slide

smoothly under last month's sheets.
The splashing of our arms lets us forget
briefly our longing for

satiated lips. Where do the deer
drink when the skies fail
to empty? The dew

is never enough for a thirst
that creates dry riverbeds of worry
as creases in our foreheads.

JOINING US IN THE WATER

a garter snake jinks, braids
      green-gold, head high, deftly
           ribbons a wake.

LA MAIN

is the river delta
to our upper limbs.
How our thoughts

diverge
  into the open
           ocean.
  How we clasp
the clock.

BURNING

On the snowy
coastal trail
we speculate
that the couple
who just breezed by

(their voices almost recognizable)
only recently fell in love
for the woman talks intensely
and the man nods in unison
to her words, listening—

their energy tangible
to be envied
until we catch up to them
at the lookout:
Oksana and Sacha, friends

of friends. We already
know their story.
They've probably been talking
about how all
their possessions

her grandmother's furniture
burned in storage. After the fire
they abandoned
their plan to travel
to Tashkent. Oksana feared

that with no belongings
to lure her home
she'd be perpetually
lost. They longed now only
to be surrounded

by family and friends. Do our
lives always become more
than we imagined? In the fire
the double bed burned.
The love between

Oksana's grandparents lasted
for over sixty years. Our love
already more
than twenty.
Our bed with its view

over the ocean
and on many nights the surf
thunders against the shore
so that we feel the vibrations
through the earth.

FLOATS

I found the coast
storm-strewn
with French books

fallen overboard,
when I walked
the shore

years ago,
pages open
to the breeze.

Ragged, worn
and wet, I took
a book home

and I still enjoy
the essence
of those pages

where we share
the best
and embrace

the worst, but
where the best floats
to the surface.

NORTH SEA CITY FOREST

BARN OWLS

At five in the morning
I'm in front of
the kitchen window

holding a glass
of water. I look out
at the dark silhouette

of the single fir tree
and suddenly
see a barn owl

its heart-shaped
face gazing
in at me. The tree

is rooted
in our new neighbour's
garden.

Where we breathe
green-calm
he sees dead needles

bird droppings
and fells
the tree down.

The city forest is
nearby and at times
we still hear the long

harsh screams
or purring calls
but we'll never again

stare
straight into
a barn owl's pupils.

BLACK EARTH

During our winter crisis
late at night I stood up
and played **Fazıl** Say's

Black Earth for you
and by chance
shortly after he came

to our city. We were seated
apart, the concert sold out
and after we shared

how we both had wept
(how could we not) when
Black Earth was his encore.

We lingered with the audience
in the aisles and how
could any of us have known

it would be our last
live concert for years, how hard
we would have to work

to keep
the music alive
in our minds

and how that autumn
we started whistling
one of us pausing

as the other
picked up
the notes.

MIDNIGHT

During a hot night in June
we stare at the empty
space beneath the tall

trees and you say, *Did
they doff their caps
and leave?* For years

they sprouted near
the art gallery entrance
enormous on the grass

in iridescent red, blue, and green.
A plaque said *Mushrooms
by Sylvie Fleury* but

if you were observant
the stalks were clearly testis, corpora
and glans. As we stand

in their abandoned space
the June bugs fly
in such abundance

around us we can hear
the music of their wings
as they soar past

our ears.
We cycle off without lights
for we've been locked

indoors so long
our batteries have died but even
in the dark

on the edge
of the path
we can see the daisies

with their wide
open faces.
A June bug

crashes
into your forehead and lands
on your right shoulder

and we laugh,
preoccupied. We're of course
both thinking of

the beauty of your
penis minus
its bright cap.

RHODODENDRON BUSH

We're in the room
that shelters

the homeless
and us lovers

an occasional
lost dog

and once
a lost child.

SUNLIGHT

Your arm over
my shoulder, my leg
over your hip

my hand on your face
the sunlight touching
our foreheads until

the rains begin
but the room
retains the light.

THE LONG MARRIAGE

As we watch
two people in wetsuits
getting washed

over by waves
you say to me,
You would

love that: a catamaran
moving smoothly
through the water.

TRAINS STILL ARRIVE

on the same
schedule

forty years later.
Laughing

I'm holding cherry
blossoms

though neither of
us

arrives nor departs
today.

REUNION OF TWO LOVERS

Meet me in the field
where the branches

of the white
willow and the dawn

redwood almost
touch. Time

has been bleak
and long during

these hours since I last
kissed you at noon.

Will we again hear
the yaffle and the klü

klü of the green
woodpecker?

LANTERNS

In the glass vase on the large white
table between us, the orange-red
papery husks of the Japanese lantern

plant are flares under floating-in-air
thoughts, and weeks and years
later when the colourful seed

coverings have crumbled
the lanterns will remain as a filigree
of our former selves.

MUCH DEPENDS UPON

us aging lovers
kissing

in autumn rain
under

a red umbrella
glazed

with melting white
hail.

LATE

Mornings we wake
hungry and thirsty, and leap

fast and straight into
the day.

Late afternoon we meet
when the light is sifted

by the gold-thread curtain
when the shadows

are not yet long, there
in our large pine bed.

WINGS

WHEN WINGS OPEN DOORS

The buzzard lands
with a thud in front
of my feet. It claws

and clutches the vole
among the leaves, then swivels
its gaze briefly at me before

flying off
in a rush
of wingspan.

A flicker
fell down
my chimney

years ago
when I was living
in a coastal

forest. I heard
steady tapping
from inside

the woodstove.
When I opened
the door latch

the flicker
flew into
my kitchen

as I raced
to open the storm
door.

Why did the buzzard land
unafraid at my feet
in the urban forest?

The flicker
enclosed in the dark
must have known

terror, but kept
tapping
while I listened.

WINDOWS

The bars on the windows
look like a prison but
you say you don't see them

and they make
you feel safe: no one
can steal

your harpsichord. You video
tour me through
your apartment: no

balcony.
You haven't felt
the wind

in your hair
for eight weeks.
As you stand

next to the open
window you say softly,
Did you hear

it? Did you
hear the serin
singing?

—2020 Madrid

CHANCE

Air entered the window
as suddenly the breeze changed.
The paper angel

I'd accordion-folded
from musical scores
swung

from the window latch
and started to float and rustle
against the frame.

I longed
to be able to read
music, and by chance

my neighbour
said, *May I store
my piano in your*

living room?
Asking around
I found a teacher

and in my mid-forties
I started to learn how
to read the scores

that unfold years
later into the beauty
of song—a sound

I can finally
feel beneath
my fingertips.

WINGS OF VOORLINDEN

Inside the locked
library, a lead book is laid open
with small warplanes

spilling out of the pages
and onto the floor.
In a far

room the black
and white wings
of a snow goose

are in the paper
drawer.
The vleugel

plays itself, keys
depressed and lifting, hammer
heads in motion

all in a room
filled with empty
red chairs.

The last child
in a yellow sweater
sits alone on the floor

next to the open
doors of empty
white lockers

their keys
hanging
untouched.

WHEN THE SALONS ARE SHUTTERED

The artist Pillan makes a bird's nest out of his pubic hair
for me. Years ago (ex-lover) Etty found a nest in a tree created
by solitary vireos from the hair of her setter. The art gallery

is closed, has been closed for months, and the carousel door
of its own accord has been spinning round and round
for days: I look through the glass and am startled

to find inside seven grey cages with seven canaries hopping
from perch to perch. Are they singing? Yesterday the vleugel
arrived and I opened its wing. My new neighbour slipped

the score of The Beatles' "Blackbird" under my door but
it stays silent beneath my fingers. I play *Songs Without Words*.
I've not (yet) met Pillan but he frequently retweets most

of my thoughts. When I tidied my hair this morning
my wooden comb broke: it had been strong for years.
I sharpen the end of a feather and start to write Etty.

OVER THE EDGE

Cycling fast through the city forest
I watch two swans take flight
as if the sun shone only

to highlight their bodies
and later the lighting man
asks me, *What are your wishes?*

and I say, *Will I at times
be in darkness?*
and he says, *I will always*

spot you, and I was bright
blind for the entire
time but I could see

your eyes over
the edge
of the piano.

THE STARVING

Behind the orangery's
closed shutters we stand

among the palm trees, and two
pianos. We talk deeply until

a woman flings open
the floor-to-ceiling windows

and we begin. Our music floods
the garden. Berio's *Wasserklavier*—

For the first time in over
sixty years all four

cacti are flowering: nectar
for the starving bees.

You know the flowering
from your youth. A woman

asks how it feels when
we perform in this heat

and I say, laughing, *It gives
me an intense headache.*

Dawning of Dusk

MORNING

My love fed our three horses
at dawn and tended our
flowers: Suzanne

with her dark eyes
hiding in the vines, the opening
of the golden-orange

sleep-caps, and the blue-jay
blooms with their large blowy
heads. Up most of the night

working on my new score
I awake late and find
my notes floating above

all the petals or do
the pitches descend down?
Light in its fullness

both fades and brightens
the musical colours.
What is the best

breath and length for
this chord? Each note
scales its own height.

AFTERNOON

Do you remember how
we stood on the steps
with scarves wrapped

around our necks? Our
friends blew soap bubbles
into the air. Midday

and the light was already fading
on the coldest and almost
shortest day of

the year. Oh, but we
were of course
warm as we held

hands and our
loved ones
cheered.

NIGHT

At dusk the rooster
jumps onto the branch
of the magnolia tree. The light

fades over the pond
and the islet in the middle
(created by hauling bucket

after bucket of sand into
the water's centre) becomes
a silhouette and is only

one of many
built or unbuilt or
yet-to-be-built shelters

for our love.
In the dark our memories
sustain the sounds of

our days—the rustle
as the horses nudge
their hay and on

our rooftop the black
bird gifts us the riff
and lilt of its song.

Slowly the stars begin
their designs as we worry
at the tapestry of our

thoughts: this light
that travels through
our infinity of years.

GEOMETRIES OF LIGHT

ZOO

Sättijan's first words
are giraffe and la Lune.
As we walk

past our neighbour's windows
under the moonlight
we peer in and see a lamp

in the shape of a giraffe
its head looking up
over the lampshade.

At the nearby vet's
a polar bear is splayed out
on the table

having its belly shaved
for tests, and we ask each other
How did they get her in there?

Octopuses
in the Antarctic
are revealed

to have merged genetically
from opposite sides
of the ice plate

meaning a gazillion years ago
there was a massive
thaw. Sättijan

finds both of our
phones and holds
one in each hand

mimicking us
talking to each other
while the world melts

into a puddle at her feet.
Late at night we find
the man-in-the-moon's reflection

in the water
as he searches
for Sättijan.

STAR SILT

We've breathed
through grey
for the past

three months
and we've
forgotten

how to squint
towards a brighter
sky.

If the stars
have been leaving
their silt

in our dreams
we've failed
to observe

their falling
light hidden
constantly

behind cloud.
When finally
visible

we may believe
the stars nest
in the darkness

of many galaxies
but physicists know
various

wavelengths of light
beyond the ability
of our vision.

LEIDEN

Sunset clouds have tangled
themselves too early in the stone
fruit trees. The snowdrops

have barely left their bulbs.
The tauntingly high
temperatures may still

slip towards a dangerous
frosting. How much earlier
can spring begin? The winter light

remains low in this city
where the citizens
chose between

a tax-free year or a lasting
university. Centuries later
students continue to think

and thrive while many street doors
lure them in with brimming
cups, or baubles.

Wooden boats anchor
at the canal edge.
The mast riggings sway

in the low breeze.
In the fifteen hundreds
Leiden was saved

from the siege
when boats sailed
in over the strategically flooded

fields. Soon the light
will lengthen and stretch
our thoughts. We can sail

over flooded land
but for crops to flourish
the water must be held

at bay. The heavy winter rains
have brought
the water table too close

to the roots.
I stare into a single
rose-soft blossom.

BLUE LIGHT

A slim woman stands
in a baby pool, no water.
She wears a wetsuit,

swim cap, and in her left
hand grasps a pully looped
over the swing set.

She mimics the front
crawl. A great blue
heron swoops low

over our silent
highway. An inflated
blue sofa moulds

the curved shape of
our curly-haired neighbour
on his front

lawn. Under our
unscratched sky
the air is brisk, clear.

Spaced apart
we sit near
the backyard pond

surrounded by
empties:
Blue Light.

—2020

WINDOWPANES

Jenny left me half
of a third.
In 1967

when she was born
Colville painted
a man looking out

over the Pacific
and behind him
on the table is a gun.

If I place my hand
on my neighbour's windowpane
I can almost touch

the back of his head
as I walk by each evening
at street level

while he's watching his large
screen TV and next
to it is a neon sign:

Fuck it. Let's buy stuff.
On his table
is a white plate

holding a white pistol.
Then one evening
he's absent but the neon

remains bright
and empty
whisky glasses

sit on the side
table.
    Roses

lean over
the sidewalk
their heads

full with the weight
of their beauty.
The bare

torso of the man
in Colville's painting
takes on

the light of
day. What
choices

do we imagine
for him or
my neighbour?

I wish I could
imagine
Jenny's story

but all I have is
her handwritten
will.

GLINT

What am I to do with this
light? How the leaves
of the poplar are so silver

among the glint of
the rowan berries
as an elderly man lies

bleeding on the bike path.
When police
and ambulance home

in on him
there's not only a dark
cloud but a murmur

as the starlings lift
in the dunes
at dusk.

GEOMETRIES OF LIGHT

At night in the dark room
I saw a gold ring of
light. I knew this was a sign:

the doctor
put drops into my eyes
and stared deep. She saw

the eye-fluid pulling
loose but the retina
was not torn, not this

time. That afternoon
you sat on the bare floor
of my new apartment

leaning against the bedroom wall
surrounded
by your chosen

triangle of sunlight.
I photographed you, relaxed and open
your hands clasped

over your right knee.
We were in a northern
country in the winter

but you find
light wherever you
go. I know this now.

We were strangers when
we watched a young woman
die, but you poured

laughter into our
conversation and the sorrow
briefly lifted. I started to pay close

attention
to you then and when
the balance-

nerve in my right inner
ear ceased to function
you visited me week after

week until many
months later my vision
and balance are again safe

and my home is no longer
loose swaying planks. The stairs
are sturdy and the light

cascades among
the treads of
our footsteps.

THE LINING

Your grandfather's winter
coat is what you wore
when we met. The buttons
restored by you, each a unique

colour, the coat golden brown
the lining torn. From the beginning
we talked deeply.
I said, *I want to die*

first. You said, *I don't want*
to die. In the zombie
movies people take
their lives. They

don't want to wait
to be eaten. But why
would you want
to die without knowing

the ending? I thought
about this for the many
weeks when we almost
lost each other

in the back and forthing of
messaging, phone calls
and (desperate) our hand
written letters

as we combined the centuries
all in one. And then
we fell into silence
where our love

for each other
rested quiet as if
we knew you needed
to build up strength

(we didn't know!) for
what lay ahead.
Before the news
reached you

we sorted shards
documented the dust.
We sewed
and repaired the lining.

Your sister
whom I never met
took her life
this September.

YIELD

The yield sign
casts a shadow:
an elongated

arrow pointing
me in the right direction.
I walk on the edge

of ponds searching
for golden leaves
washed against

the shore. I saw them
just the other day
and they reminded

me of our walk
after you lost
your sister.

I'd taken a photo back
then and wanted
to take another one

but time doesn't yield
for our longings.
The leaves are now

submerged
and blue-winged teals
feed at the deep-gold border.

GRIEVING

Each night on
the deserted streets

the empty number
thirty bus, all lit up,

drives past us
once again

as we walk in
the pouring rain.

BOWL

In her rose
dress she cycles
while

he rides
the carrier.
He wants to take

a selfie
but needs both
hands to hang

on. They're
searching
for a broken

bowl healed
with gold
to gift

to their grieving
friend. He's an organist
and she's a northern

nurse: she mends
the broken
bones of gold

miners
when their sky
falls in.

CLARITY

The purple and yellow croci
forcing their way out

of the ground are undelivered
messages from the dead.

What are words but
incomprehensible jumblings

of the alphabet? If we want
clarity we should try casting

a bronze sculpture: buried
it might survive a thousand years.

But what is a thousand when
we speak of millennia? We move

forwards or backwards
in time, and in this brevity

we carve the names
into stone of beloved

lost friends: they remind us
of our inabilities.

NIGHT ALIGNMENTS

TENDING

I've forgotten
the order. Was the chain
on our gate cut

first, gently looped
back as if it was still whole?
Or did we find the first

of multiple soiled scraps of fabric
near the gate? One morning
we found the wooden mailbox

smashed. On a torrential rain day
our express parcel was left
by a neighbour to soak

in the middle
of our driveway.
Twice the police

arrive after receiving
anonymous calls:
we're drug dealers

or cruel to our animals.
The officers don't stay long.
Our friends come

round for a refreshing
drink. When they leave
we're again alone.

NIGHT ALIGNMENTS

This is the latest era
of night alignments.
Each new moon

spills forth
the clearest
stars

and since no moonbeams will glint
off their wingtips
the sky is ideal for the soaring

of war jets. Are those
constellations or the glister
of hell? We never know

until it's too late.
And then it takes lifetimes
to learn how to swallow

the fire. Six generations later
memory
will be of wounds not healing

and of sterile gauze
like promises fallen
from the skies.

BLOOM

Women hand out
sunflower seeds

to trespassing soldiers
so that when they

die on land
that is not their own

flowers will bloom
from their bodies.

THESE ARE THE OBJECTS

What is spilling
from his cloth bag?
A photograph in the grass

portrays a young girl.
In our quick glance
metal cylinders

look like crayons.
The soldier's hands
are clasped

as if holding more
than this
        moment.

Postage stamps are waiting
to be sent or received
but from a tobacco tin

they too slip onto the grass.
A note is a crumpled ball:
what are the words

the soldier wrote?
These are the objects left
after the plunder, the ones only

our loved ones
value. His body
in the grass.

SECRET CODE

Freed from prison
Diet Kloos-Barendregt
borrowed a bike and cycled
                          to Amsterdam.
Wavy brown hair, glasses
and a determined look
she stood
day after day outside
Jan's prison window
and whistled
their secret
code.
     Childhood playmates
they reunited when
they worked
together
in the underground.
                         Two weeks
after their wedding
they were hauled
out of bed
by a twelve-man team
on charges
of espionage.
Beaten and tortured, Jan
sustained

her innocence.
               Diet organized
illegal house concerts
found food and underground
addresses
for Jewish families
transported
illegal pamphlets
and weapons
and visited
people in hiding.
                  For the rest
of her life she carried
Jan's last
letter and his photo in her purse:
                             long-legged
and blond, he sits casually leaning
against a tree.

BLACKBIRDS AND GREENFINCHES

At sunset in the forest
I hear the migratory birds
that Jan Kloos recorded

in his notebook.
Banned from
his biology studies

he joined the resistance
and found cover work
as an ornithologist.

His last
      letter to his wife
was smuggled out

of prison:
pencil written
on a thin sheet

of paper, and
folded to fit
into the palm of

her hand.
      I have
no regrets

for everything
I did.
      You taught

me to be happy while
I also know
I gave

you happiness.
She carried
on

with music:
her life as
a celebrated

contralto.
I'll think about
you

until
the last
moment.

INVENTORY

of her personal
possessions. Boxes stacked
on the floors. She's told
she can't ship her teas.

She thinks of bonfires, of leaving
the past behind. How many
books of knowledge
have the victors burned?

Yes, she says, *the boxes
are heavy. Yes, they all
contain stories*.

She throws her matches
away. She sets the kettle
on the stove.

HISTORY

doesn't repeat itself
but sometimes

like a dog circling round
chasing after

its own tail, it starts
to gnaw until

it's suddenly faced
with a hole.

ENTER

In the early hours of
the morning thousands
of large vehicles enter
the city blowing sirens

and horns. We're all
suddenly wide awake. Most
of us are always home, day and
night (by choice

of course). Our
meals are delivered
to our doors. Many, many years ago
the frail and elderly confined

to their homes had a meals-on-wheels
program or so I'm told.
The drivers of the heavy tractors
head into the city centre. These farmers,

many of them older, are among
the few of us who still venture
outdoors. They want to remind us where
our food comes from

though most of our fruits
and vegetables, like us, are now
grown indoors in vertical
gardens.

HESITATIONS

Stained glass windows
are backlit and from the upper
floor we hear last year's

choir music. A blue
Citroën passes us twice on
the abandoned street.

The security guard
with his chain of keys
opens the door

of the clinic.
At the corner we listen
as I stare up

at the treetops
and you look
down at your feet.

From behind curtains
we hear a pianist
at play. Even her

hesitations
uplift us. A girl
stops to kiss

a boy
on his bike
before they part racing

home. We run
in the opposite
direction and hide

in the children's playground.
Moments later a police
cube-van finds the street.

BLUR

Flowers were the word blur.
She was always moving
too fast. Years

later when the majority
wanted to stay
safe inside

she slipped out
the back door
with her white

cane. Flowers
were the scent she followed.
All the colour

in the world
was gone. The police
stopped her

and asked, *Is this walk
urgent?*
She said, It's the last

day of my life.
Name and age?
and then the pause.

You're one hundred and four?
Yes, she said, and waving
his hand he said, *Go.*

AT PLAY

A mother shows
her child how to throw
the red leaves into the air

so she can capture
the image. Years later the manual
for mental illness lists staring

at trees, chasing clouds, skipping
pebbles over ponds, and stargazing
with dawn or dusk or midnight

as subcategories. Childhood
illnesses encompass playing
with leaves or pinecones or

mud. Photos are included.

MODEL COLLAPSE

If you and I are in the minority
and/or create a rare idea
then artificial intelligence will

treat us like a petit
basset griffon vendéen
versus a golden retriever

where gold is
over-represented, until
trained on too many

self-generated golden
ideas, the end result
will be images not of

unique dogs, humans
or ideas but self-generated
golden blobs.

WHAT IS LEFT IS

the glow at the
bottom of
the tin bowl

after the muskrat
has licked
the milk clean.

SHAPE

Poseidon in a sideways
stance is ready to hurl
his absent trident. One

of two cleaners
hesitates before she dusts
his penis

with her soft cloth.
Does he lack his trident
as a security measure?

Accidentally a poet slips
in and sketches the scene
with her eyes: Supreme

Headquarters Allied Powers
Europe: what sculptural
shape will our future take?

SCULPTURE

He sketches wind turbines
and enters abandoned
buildings. Lays down partial
floorboards. Cuts

holes in walls. Avoids
military conscription.
Avoids jail. He forgets his identity
card at home. Avoids getting

arrested. Smuggles
white canvas into the derelict
buildings. He wears paint splattered
sandals, and walks softly.
She never knows when he's out

or in. He calls her his Russian: her waist
length hair, green eyes. Cooks her cups of tea.
Asks her, *Why do you only paint faces?*
Collects burgundy and green

rocks for her. Cuts
cactuses and sets them out on ceramic
plates. Waits for her to find human shapes
in the plants, in the stones.

ENTANGLEMENTS

BODIES OF WORK

Two arched windows
and four arched mirrors
stretch the space

in the round room
in Rodin's house
while a visitor lies

in a bed on wheels.
Her own square mirror
projects the sculptures

and for once we forget
to look at images and reflections
of ourselves.

Centauress
has an elongated
upper body

and the legs
of a horse.
Nude Eve

twines her arms
around her torso.
Covered

by layers
of multi-hued
quilts

the woman in her bed
is the only traveller
who smiles expansively

beneath the serious gaze
of her orange-haired
lover.

ART OPTIONS

In a mason's yard
by Putney Bridge
cast-offs stolen

by a young artist
who carved intimacy
from marble:

Samson and Delilah
now stored under
glass. Outside

the gallery's stone walls
lovers pry open their minds
by manoeuvring

around reclining person
(in two parts)
while a young couple

by the riverbank
loosen their
embrace.

THE UNWRITTEN BOOK

When he cycles past her
studio at night he sees the silhouette
of her indoor tree, the leaves in shadow
on the pane. He doesn't
see her, but knows

she's most certainly there
holding an unwritten book in her thoughts
like a burning flame.
He wants her to be the one
who has strewn

the trail of live embers
to his bed where he continues
to turn the pages, and where his sheets
are dusty from the black
soot on his hands, on his soles.

STARSTRUCK

In Memory of Mark Strand

Freshly showered after
the power outage
in his pink shirt

Mark reads to us
on the patio. Vines
from the trellis send

their tendrils into
our hair. Candles
flicker on the railing.

Latecomers rustle in the bushes
trying to get closer.
Mark talks about a trip

to Shut-in Island:
in his childhood the skiff's plug
was accidentally kicked loose—

two women waiting on shore
half the night for
their husbands and children.

The long row home surrounded
by the last of the sperm
whales. Bailing and

bailing until in the dark
the plug was found and the sinking
stopped. Tonight

not even the housecats
are shut in. They sneak past
the damp perspiring legs of

their owners, prowl in a ring
on the edge of the listeners. After
the reading we watch Mark

eat blueberry shortcake. The table
is cleared. Candlewicks sit low
in their wax

and it is time. We drive
through fog
and then through lightning.

My lover
asks, *In the movie world
how would the poet compare?*

He's in the stratosphere.
Like Clint Eastwood?
Yes, like him riding his horse

in the desert
near Mojácar.
I'll send you

a postcard.
I'll be there next month
wearing

a skirt
pink shirt
and spurs.

ANIMALS

Along the distant beach the horse carries her through
the rising surf. Her lover waits. She's his restless

adventurer, a horse her ascendant
sign, or so she always says. When she returns home

months later they sit at the breakfast table.
I hear a horse neighing, he says, startled.

From her kitchen window the trees crowd
his view. *Yes*, she says, *two horses live on the edge*

of the forest. He shakes his head
glad that no tigers, her dominant sign, stalk

about in the backyard. When they walk along the shore
she points to the shoals: *the horse,*

the mare and the colt, she says. He's a botanist,
unused to mammals, and prefers to guide

her away from the animals.
Along the barrens he teaches her the names

of the rare plants. Star Flower: whorl
of leaves and seven white petals. She points to rose

orchids, tiny as her thumb nail.
He pauses and says, *Dragon's Mouth*.

Ah, she says. *Let me taste
the dragon's mouth*, and they're back

again on her astrological ark
paired two by two: the tiger

and the dragon.

Sailor

WHEN A FRIEND LENDS A POET MOVIES

Like the gap in the wall behind
the filing cabinet that hides a tunnel
into John Malkovich's brain,
the door at the head of the poet's bed
leads directly into her control
centre: hum of green
lights, a large blue ball,
a red kneeling chair, a globe
of the upside down world
showing Oceania.

A sailor sleeps in the poet's bed
while she bounces on the blue
ball. Words scroll down the face
of her turquoise Apple.
With her mouse as guide, poems vanish
and her Apple plays movies.
After her sailor wakes up
she tells him, *You're not allowed
into my brain
without kissing me first.*

WHEN LOVE IS AN INCINERATOR

In the spa she shows
her sailor how
to hang his swim

suit on the hook.
A naked man whips
a white towel

over the hot coals
and the heat surrounds
them like summer's

exhalation. Pool-dipped
they walk the path
of stones. The ocean

and a pebbled beach
almost fit in the palm of
her hand. Later their touch

lasts all night
while outside
the air

remains muddy
even though Hundertwasser
overhauled

the incinerator.
Her sailor laughs
at the red-blue

striped hat
super-sized over the ventilation
shaft

as they continue to breathe
shared
air.

GREAT CIRCLE ROUTE

At night the soundings
as the bolts from the castle gate
slide into their locks.

She dreams a person is flailing
underwater, the air bubbles
rising slowly, only she's uncertain

whether it's she or her lover
drowning. That night his ship
crosses the Arctic Circle.

In the castle retreat
she eats upside-down cake
from a bowl engraved HMS *Hero*.

Where did her patron
find these dishes and what happened
to the sailors who used

them? So many of her lover's days
she longs to envision—his sea bunk
where he harnesses himself in shifts.

Slipping away from the castle
she walks to the nearest village
while her sailor on an unscheduled port call

to Bodo strolls the wharf.
Both find phone booths
so that along the ocean depths

words become encoded into light
and at 12.23.06 simultaneously
the message signals blink.

ALL LIT UP

She's driving at night
through a white-out
when suddenly

a phone booth appears
all lit up in the middle of
nowhere. She begs

the operator, says the coin
slot's all iced over
and could she please put her call

through. And the operator
does. The duty officer
on board the ship says, sure

she can come
down to the harbour
if she brings

maple donuts.

WHILE KISSING ONBOARD

Her black & white snap
shot of his sink labelled

(weirdly) *sink*. Obviously
not anything by Duchamp.

Certainly a deterrent:
pissing forbidden

but vomiting
is permissible.

Shore Leave

RAIN

The wind billows
the back of your coat
as the exhausted farmer

fantasizes about sleeping
in his hammock. His sunflowers
grow in the long

run of the fields
as I stand on your toes
kissing you. Single

raindrops start
to fall onto your nose.
Only the woman

grazing her horse
under the trees, smells
the rain on the leaves.

THE BLISS OF STORM ECCENTRICITIES

The sky churns
in a confusion of
blue-grey clouds

as we cycle towards
the sea. A woman walks alone
pushing

a wheelchair. A couple
climbs over the electric wire
fence marked *No trespassing*

and their camouflage clothing
blurs into the green-dung
landscape of the dunes.

A man stoops low
over the trail and talks
to a toad

hopping a slow path
to the opposite
side. We're heading straight

into the shore of a storm.
When the raindrops begin
to whisper into the sand

we fling our arms wide
and walk barefoot
over the shells.

FLEETING

The heavy fruit
falls into the miniature wild
flower meadow outside
the bedroom window.

Without my glasses all I see is a blur
of leaf blades and sun-orange
as I feel your breathing
against my right shoulder.

Your warm hand cups
my sea-cooled left breast
while the iron monger outside
drives by loud-speakering

but the bed is made of olive wood
and we have no metal scraps
to give away.
Braided and salt-stained

string is tied around
our wrists. *No one eats
the oranges
that grow in this city*

you say as church bells
chime our fleeting hours
and rain falls briefly
refreshing the street-side oleander.

OPEN GATES

I cycled to the French bakery
but heading home a marathon race
blocked my route so I diverted via

the sea. By chance I passed the cemetery
where I'd told you the writers
Elizabeth and Agatha were buried

in the same grave, dying within twelve
days of each other in 1804. I took
a photo for you and stood and stared

at the wrought iron gate and found
a tiny street library next to
the entrance: *Please take books*

for free. By the time I reached the sea
the tide had crept
in and I cycled on the wavy edge

of surf, tires crunching
the shells. Eventually I had to turn
inland so I asked a stranger

to carry my new library
as I hoisted my bike through deep
drifts of sand. At the top of

the hill on a weathered bench
I ate your breakfast and wondered
who Agatha and Elizabeth were and how

they came to rest together
for over two centuries in a world
wishing to tear apart, murder or

imprison people because of their
love. Ah, I ate your favourite
pear and chocolate tart out there

under the unfurling sky
with Heisenberg's *Schritte über Grenzen*
in my lap. It tasted almost

as if you were right
there beside me
as if we were sharing.

ACKNOWLEDGMENTS

Northern Childhood (a selection of ten poems from *Northern Bush*) was a finalist for the CBC (Canadian Broadcasting Corporation) Poetry Prize, 2024.

"Dawning of Dusk" was commissioned by the Greek composer Panos Gklistis. For soprano, clarinet, and piano, the three love songs were premiered by the Bosklank trio in 2024.

"Zoo" received an Arc Award of Awesomeness honourable mention in May 2024.

"Taiga" was a winner in the Poem in Your Pocket Day Contest, League of Canadian Poets, 2023.

"Blue Light" (under the former title "Sambro") received an Arc Award of Awesomeness honourable mention in December 2020.

With immense thanks to the following publications where some of the poems in *Rush of Wingspan* were published (often in earlier versions and sometimes under alternative titles).

"Flight into Puppetry" in *The Antigonish Review*.

"Ashes" in *Dreamcatcher* (UK).

"Taiga" in *Poem in Your Pocket Day Brochure* plus as a postcard designed by Megan Fildes (League of Canadian Poets).

"Ancestors" in *Periodicities*.

"Floats" in *Periodicities*.

"Blue Light" in *talking about strawberries all of the time*.

"Windowpanes" in *talking about strawberries all of the time*.

"The Lining" in *Stand Magazine* (UK).

"Bowl" in *talking about strawberries all of the time*, and *Poetry Pause* (League of Canadian Poets.)

"Bloom" in *The New Quarterly*.

"Enter" in *Periodicities*.

"Blur" in *The Time After: An Anthology of Atlantic Canada*. (League of Canadian Poets).

"At Play" in *The New Quarterly*.

"Sculpture" in *Prism International* and in *Poetry Pause* (League of Canadian Poets).

"When a Friend Lends a Poet Movies" in *I Found it at the Movies* (Guernica Editions).

I wish to thank: Allan Hepburn, Joanne Pisano, Jennifer Roberts, Lisa Quinn, Jonathan Crago, Jacqueline Davis, Kathleen Fraser, Lisa Aitken, Nina Ballerstedt, and all the wonderful people at McGill-Queen's University Press for the essential work they do on behalf of authors. Bird migration scientist Jamie McLaren for his invaluable advice. All my amazing friends for the encouragement and joy they add to my life. Bruce for his ongoing belief, friendship, support, love, and encouragement. And in memory of Hannah Wertheim: her strength, intelligence, humour, and kindness are deeply missed.

"Weasels" is for Valentijn.

"Tools" is for Colleen and Paul.

"Keening" is for Chris and Seana.

"Kindness" is for Wouter.

"Barn Owls" is for Jamie.

"When Wings Open Doors" is for Meike.

"Windows" is for Jorge.

"Wings of Voorlinden" is for Alexander.

"When the Salons Are Shuttered" is for Kathy.

"Dawning of Dusk" is for Panos and Teus Jan.

"Zoo" is for Nicolas and Gulzhan.

"Secret Code" is for Joachim.

"Blackbirds and Greenfinches" is for Kees.

"Model Collapse" is for Chris V.

"Bodies of Work" is for Rob.

"When a Friend Lends a Poet Movies" is for Nancy C.

"Fleeting" is for Michalis.

"Open Gates" is for Herma.

NOTES

PENELOPE: Penelope Fitzgerald (1916–2000) was a British writer.

BLACK EARTH: Fazıl Say (1970) is a Turkish composer and concert pianist.

MUCH DEPENDS UPON: written as a parallel poem to "The Red Wheelbarrow" by American poet William Carlos Williams (1883–1963).

WINGS OF VOORLINDEN: *Dat rosa miel apibus* (2009) is by the German artist Anselm Kiefer (1945). *The Wings Are in the Paper Drawer* (1972/1973) is by American artist Robert Kinmont.

WHEN THE SALONS ARE SHUTTERED: *Songs without Words* is solo piano music by the German composer Felix Mendelssohn (1809–1847). Vleugel is the Dutch word for grand piano and wing of a bird.

THE STARVING: *Wasserklavier* (Waterpiano) is a two-piano work by Italian composer Luciano Berio (1925–2003).

STAR SILT: written while listening to a track of the same name by Two Deep Breaths (Australian composers Ashley Hribar on piano, and Richard Vaudrey on cello).

WINDOWPANES: *Pacific* (1967) is a painting by the Canadian artist Alex Colville (1920–2013).

THESE ARE THE OBJECTS: Inspired by the photograph *Fallen North Vietnamese Soldier* (1968) from British photographer Don McCullin (1935). *Hearts of Darkness: Photographs by Don McCullin* (New York: Alfred A. Knopf, 1981), 41.

SECRET CODE: Diet Kloos-Barendregt was a Dutch contralto and resistance fighter (1924–2015). In 2017 she was posthumously honoured by Yad Vashem with the title Righteous Among the Nations. As a non-Jew, with her life, freedom, and safety at risk, and with no financial motives, she chose to save the lives of Jews. At least six people were saved by her work. Post-war she had a brief relationship with the poet Paul Celan.

BLACKBIRDS AND GREENFINCHES: Jan Kloos was a Dutch violinist, biologist, and resistance fighter (1919–1945). Jan's letter to Diet was viewed on February 26, 2011 at the Vrijheidsmuseum, Netherlands, as part of the exhibit *Diet Kloos and Paul Celan: Mijn Stem Overleefde*. Translation of Jan's letter is by Eleonore Schönmaier.

MODEL COLLAPSE: based on an article by Emily Wenger. "AI Returns Gibberish When Trained on Too Much AI-Generated Data," *Nature* 631 (2024): 742–3.

ART OPTIONS: *Samson and Delilah* (1913) is by French artist Henri Gaudier-Brzeska (1891–1915). *The Embracers* is an alternative name for the same sculpture. *Two Piece Reclining Figure* (1968) is by English artist Henry Moore (1898–1986).

STARSTRUCK: Canadian-born American poet Mark Strand (1934–2014).

WHEN A FRIEND LENDS A POET MOVIES: John Malkovich (1953) is an American actor. *Being John Malkovich* is a 1999 American film directed by Spike Jonze and written by Charlie Kaufman.

WHEN LOVE IS AN INCINERATOR: the Vienna incinerator is by the Austrian architect Friedensreich Hundertwasser (1928–2000).

GREAT CIRCLE ROUTE: the shortest course between two points on the surface of a sphere.

WHILE KISSING ONBOARD: Marcel Duchamp (1887–1968) was a French artist. His *Fountain* (1917) consists of a porcelain urinal.

OPEN GATES: Elizabeth Wolff (1738–1804) and Agatha Deken (1741–1804) were Dutch novelists who co-authored multiple books. Werner Heisenberg, *Schritte Über Grenzen* [Crossing over Borders]*: Gesammelte Reden und Aufsätze* (Munich: R. Piper & Co., 1971).

THE AUTHOR'S WEBPAGE CAN BE FOUND AT: https://eleonoreschonmaier.com

THE HUGH MacLENNAN POETRY SERIES

Editors: Allan Hepburn and Carolyn Smart

Waterglass Jeffery Donaldson
All the God-Sized Fruit Shawna Lemay
Chess Pieces David Solway
Giving My Body to Science Rachel Rose
The Asparagus Feast S.P. Zitner
The Thin Smoke of the Heart Tim Bowling
What Really Matters Thomas O'Grady
A Dream of Sulphur Aurian Haller
Credo Carmine Starnino
Her Festival Clothes Mavis Jones
The Afterlife of Trees Brian Bartlett
Before We Had Words S.P. Zitner
Bamboo Church Ricardo Sternberg
Franklin's Passage David Solway
The Ishtar Gate Diana Brebner
Hurt Thyself Andrew Steinmetz
The Silver Palace Restaurant Mark Abley
Wet Apples, White Blood Naomi Guttman
Palilalia Jeffery Donaldson
Mosaic Orpheus Peter Dale Scott
Cast from Bells Suzanne Hancock
Blindfold John Mikhail Asfour
Particles Michael Penny
A Lovely Gutting Robin Durnford
The Little Yellow House Heather Simeney MacLeod
Wavelengths of Your Song Eleonore Schönmaier
But for Now Gordon Johnston
Some Dance Ricardo Sternberg
Outside, Inside Michael Penny
The Winter Count Dilys Leman
Tablature Bruce Whiteman

Trio Sarah Tolmie
hook nancy viva davis halifax
Where We Live John Reibetanz
The Unlit Path Behind the House Margo Wheaton
Small Fires Kelly Norah Drukker
Knots Edward Carson
The Rules of the Kingdom Julie Paul
Dust Blown Side of the Journey Eleonore Schönmaier
slow war Benjamin Hertwig
The Art of Dying Sarah Tolmie
Short Histories of Light Aidan Chafe
On High Neil Surkan
Translating Air Kath MacLean
The Night Chorus Harold Hoefle
Look Here Look Away Look Again Edward Carson
Delivering the News Thomas O'Grady
Grotesque Tenderness Daniel Cowper
Rail Miranda Pearson
Ganymede's Dog John Emil Vincent
The Danger Model Madelaine Caritas Longman
A Different Wolf Deborah-Anne Tunney
rushes from the river disappointment stephanie roberts
A House in Memory David Helwig
Side Effects May Include Strangers Dominik Parisien
Check Sarah Tolmie
The Milk of Amnesia Danielle Janess
Field Guide to the Lost Flower of Crete Eleonore Schönmaier
Unbound Gabrielle McIntire
Ripping down half the trees Evan J
whereabouts Edward Carson
The Tantramar Re-Vision Kevin Irie
Earth Words: Conversing with Three Sages John Reibetanz
Vlarf Jason Camlot
Unbecoming Neil Surkan

Bitter in the Belly John Emil Vincent
unfinishing Brian Henderson
Nuclear Family Jean Van Loon
Full Moon of Afraid and Craving Melanie Power
Rags of Night in Our Mouths Margo Wheaton
watching for life David Zieroth
Orchid Heart Elegies Zoë Landale
The House You Were Born In Tanya Standish McIntyre
The Decline and Fall of the Chatty Empire John Emil Vincent
New Songs for Orpheus John Reibetanz
the swailing Patrick James Errington
movingparts Edward Carson
Murmuration: Marianne's Book John Baglow
Take the Compass Maureen Hynes
act normal nancy viva davis halifax
aboutness Eimear Laffan
twofold Edward Carson
Whiny Baby Julie Paul
Metromorphoses John Reibetanz
Bridestones Miranda Pearson
Dreamcraft Peter Dale Scott
Water Quality Cynthia Woodman Kerkham
Without Beginning or End Jacqueline Bourque
White Lily John Emil Vincent
Kingdom of the Clock: A Novel in Verse Daniel Cowper
SCAR/CITY Daniela Elza
At Beckett's Grave Robin Durnford
Empties Neil Surkan
Rush of Wingspan Eleonore Schönmaier